NEW FOR SPRING!

SCIENTIFIC BREAKTHROUGHS

DISCOVERIES IN PHYSICS that changed the world

SCIENTIFIC BREAKTHROUGHS

DISCOVERIES IN CHEMISTRY that changed the world

SCIENTIFIC BREAKTHROUGHS

DISCOVERIES IN LIFE SCIENCE that changed the world

SCIENTIFIC BREAKTHROUGHS

DISCOVERIES IN EARTH AND SPACE that changed the world

SCIENTIFIC BREAKTHROUGHS

DISCOVERIES IN MEDICINE that changed the world

BLAISE PASCAL

Blaise Pascal was born in Clermont-Ferrand, France, in 1623. At the age of 19, Pascal invented one of the first mechanical calculators to help his father's work as a tax collector. After discovering air pressure in 1648, he went on to help to create probability theory, the mathematics of chance, in 1656. He died in Paris, France, in 1662.

and measured how high up the tube the liquid went. He found it was about 30 inches (76 cm)—a 14th as high as the water in a siphon. The level of mercury rose and fell slightly from day to day. This showed that whatever force was causing the liquid to move could change.

Air pressure

After Torricelli died, Blaise Pascal took over the research. Pascal thought it was not a vacuum pulling the mercury up the tube but the weight of the air pushing down on the mercury bath and forcing the liquid to rise up the tube. In 1648 Pascal organized for a mercury tube to be carried up a mountain in central France. The height of the mercury dropped as it was taken higher. Pascal was right. At higher altitudes, there was less air to push down on the mercury, so it rose to a lower height. Pascal's

The air pressure at the top of Mount Everest is one third of the pressure at sea level.

discovery also explained the siphon limit. It was air pressure that was pushing water through siphons—and it was never strong enough to push it higher than around 33 feet (10 m). Today pressure is measured in units called Pascals (Pa).

Empty space

So what was in the space above the mercury inside the tube? Could it be nothing at all—a vacuum? In 1650, a German inventor, Otto von Guericke (1602–1686), showed that vacuums were indeed possible. He used a pump to remove all the air from inside two metal hemispheres that fitted together. The pressure pushing out from the inside was zero, and so the air pressure pushing on the outside locked the hemispheres together very tightly. Even teams of horses could not pull them apart!

Discovery number: 3

FACTS

- The pressure 330 feet (100 m) under water is 10 times higher than at the surface.
- Sound is a wave in air and so it cannot travel through a vacuum. However, light can shine through it.
- Blaise Pascal also invented the roulette wheel.

Air pressure pushed Von Guericke's hemispheres together so tightly that two teams of eight horses could not pull them apart.

12   13

Discoveries in Physics that Changed the World

SCIENTIFIC
BREAKTHROUGHS

DISCOVERIES IN
MEDICINE
that changed the world

Rose Johnson

rosen publishing's
rosen
central®

Published in 2015 by The Rosen Publishing Group, Inc.
29 East 21st Street, New York, NY 10010

First Edition

Library of Congress Cataloging-in-Publication Data
Johnson, Rose, 1981- author.
Discoveries in medicine that changed the world / Rose Johnson. -- First edition.
    pages cm. -- (Scientific breakthroughs)
 Includes bibliographical references and index.
 ISBN 978-1-4777-8611-6 (library bound)
1. Medicine--History--Juvenile literature. 2. Discoveries in science--Juvenile literature. I. Title.
 R133.5.J64 2015
 610.9--dc23
                            2014027728

Editor and Text: Rose Johnson
Editorial Director: Lindsey Lowe
Children's Publisher: Anne O'Daly
Design Manager: Keith Davis
Designers: Lynne Lennon
Picture Researcher: Clare Newman
Picture Manager: Sophie Mortimer

Brown Bear Books has made every attempt to contact the copyright holder. If anyone has any information please contact:
licensing@brownbearbooks.co.uk

All artwork: © Brown Bear Books

Manufactured in Malaysia

Contents

Introduction

The practice of medicine is as old as civilization. Ever since the dawn of history, doctors have been looking for ways to cure disease and extend life.

It is not just humans that take medicine. Chimpanzees living in the forests of Africa eat the leaves of a particular plant when they have upset stomachs. It is likely that primitive humans used herbal medicines in the same way. Experts in these remedies would have been highly respected like doctors are today. The first doctors we know about were from 5,000 years ago in Mesopotamia (now Iraq). As well as being doctors, these people were also priests, who believed that illness was caused by evil spirits in the body.

Healthcare is provided by a team of doctors, nurses, and technicians.

Sports and exercise are a good way of staying healthy and avoiding disease.

Eating the right foods is important for maintaining a healthy body.

Ancient links

All doctors working today take the Hippocratic Oath. This is a promise that they will do nothing that could make a person more ill—only try to make them better. This idea stems from a Greek doctor called Hippocrates, who lived 2,400 years ago. Hippocrates was one of the first to say that illness was caused by problems with the body, not supernatural spirits.

Understanding the body

The history of medicine relates how doctors figured out how the body works in ever greater detail, so they could identify what was causing disease. Today, there are cures for many common diseases that would have killed people in the past. Modern medicine offers the prospect of a long life, but it also shows that we have to look after our bodies to avoid developing diseases.

Surgery

Today, surgery is at the cutting edge of modern medicine, with doctors slicing into the body to fix problems. However, surgery is an ancient practice.

It may come as a surprise to hear that the earliest operations were brain surgery. Human skulls dating back to the dawn of civilization, some suggest even 14,000 years ago, have been found with a hole cut in them. This is trepanation, in which the skull was operated on to cure seizures, headaches, and mental problems. Evidence from other ancient human remains shows that people performed surgery on teeth and were able to set broken bones. Ancient writings show pictures of doctors working with knives. These were the first surgeons.

Modern surgery can last many hours. The blue-green clothes worn by surgical teams helps the surgeon to concentrate on the red colored body parts without getting tired eyes.

Surgical manual

The earliest book about surgery we know about was written by Sushruta, an Indian doctor who lived about 2,600 years ago. His writing gives instructions on how to cut open parts of the body, how to feel around inside the body, and then how to close up the cut safely using stitches or other techniques.

Modern surgery

Today's surgeons are very skilled at what they do, but about 200 years ago they were not seen as proper doctors. In many cases, people went to see the barber if they needed an operation. Barbers did everything from cutting hair to chopping off legs!

A statue of Sushruta in India honors the ancient figure as one of the founding fathers of medical science.

SUSHRUTA

No one is sure when this Indian doctor lived. He may have worked as far back as 3,000 years ago but the best guess is he lived in Varanasi in northern India around 600 BCE. He is thought to be the inventor of plastic surgery, where he used tissue taken from one part of the body to fix damage somewhere else.

Blood Circulation

Blood carries oxygen and nutrients around the body and carries away the waste. The way blood circulates was not figured out until 1628.

William Harvey discovered how blood moved around the body in the early 17th century. Before that time doctors were taught blood was made inside the heart and liver and drawn into the body where it was used up—and replaced by new blood. Harvey figured out that if this were true a person would be making 550 lb (250 kg) of blood a day!

William Harvey made drawings of the valves that he found in the veins of the forearm.

BLOOD VESSELS

William Harvey found that there are two types of blood vessel. Arteries carry blood away from the heart; veins bring it back. Valves inside the veins stop blood from flowing in the wrong direction.

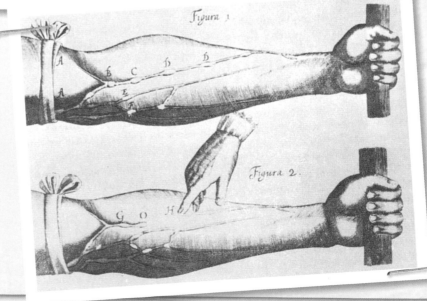

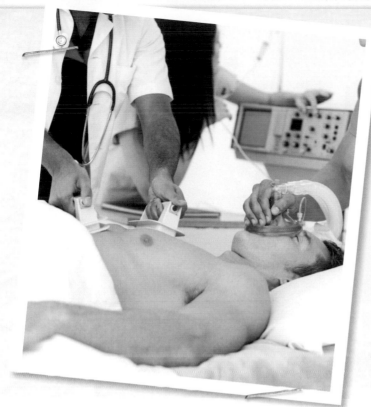

IMPLICATIONS

When a sick person arrives in an ER, the first thing a doctor does is check if a person's heart is beating. The body cannot survive if the heart stops. If the heart has stopped, the medics try to get it going again. To do this, they give it a powerful electric shock with a machine called a defibrillator.

A defibrillator restarts the electrical control system that makes the heart's muscles pump in the correct sequence.

Body pump

Harvey reasoned that the amount of blood stayed the same and was pumped around by the heart. He performed experiments to find out how the heart worked, which by today's standards would be unethical. He sliced open living animals and observed their hearts until the subjects died.

Moving blood

Harvey found that the right side of the heart received blood from the body and pumped it to the lungs. The left side (which is bigger and stronger) took the blood from the lungs and pumped it around the body.

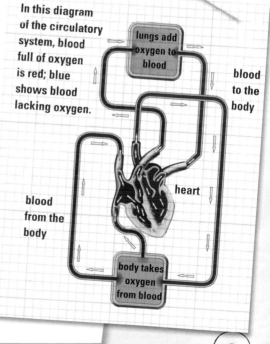

In this diagram of the circulatory system, blood full of oxygen is red; blue shows blood lacking oxygen.

lungs add oxygen to blood

blood to the body

heart

blood from the body

body takes oxygen from blood

Vaccines

Vaccines prepare the body to fight off dangerous diseases. The first vaccine tackled smallpox, a deadly disease that covered the body in sores.

Most vaccines are given by injection into the blood or muscles, while some are taken as pills.

At the end of the 18th century, smallpox killed more people than any other disease. Sufferers were covered in painful sores and nearly all died. However, in China doctors had learned how to use a weak strain of the disease to protect people. The weak strain only caused a minor illness, but it meant the body was able to defend against the more deadly form. However, these smallpox medicines sometimes killed the patients.

EDWARD JENNER

Jenner, born in 1749, grew up in the heart of England's cattle country. His vaccine discovery made him famous and he became the king's personal doctor. Jenner died in 1823.

Jenner vaccinates children against smallpox after the news of his technique spreads.

Cowpox

By the 18th century, this idea had spread to Europe. In the west of England, people noticed that dairy maids who caught cowpox, a disease similar to smallpox but less deadly, from cows were immune to smallpox. In 1774 a farmer called Benjamin Jesty injected his wife and sons with a small amount of pus from a cowpox sufferer. They caught cowpox but were safe from smallpox.

Medical test

A local doctor Edward Jenner made the first scientific study of vaccines (although that word came later). After 20 years, he was sure cowpox sufferers never caught smallpox. In 1796 Jenner put the technique to the test by vaccinating eight-year-old James Phipps with cowpox. A few weeks later he deliberately infected James with smallpox but the boy did not catch the disease— the vaccine had made him immune to smallpox.

IMPLICATIONS

In 1966, a worldwide vaccination program was set up to wipe out smallpox completely. Medics rushed to outbreaks of the diease all over the world, vaccinating everyone in the area. That stopped the disease from spreading. The last case of smallpox was in Somalia in 1977.

Anesthetics

An anesthetic is a chemical that decreases a person's awareness of what is happening, reducing the pain they feel and making them fall asleep.

In 1799, English chemist Sir Humphry Davy (1778–1829) discovered that breathing a gas called nitrous oxide stopped him feeling pain—it also made him feel good and laugh a lot. The gas is now known as "laughing gas." Davy suggested that the gas might have medical uses—although his idea was ignored. However, laughing gas is used today by dentists and doctors as a mild anesthetic.

FACTS

- The word *anesthetic* means "without perception."
- In the early 1800s, people held ether and nitrous oxide parties.
- During a general anesthetic, where the patient is unconscious, doctors also administer muscle relaxants so the patient cannot move.

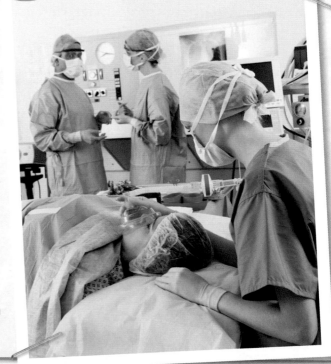

Anesthetics are administered by a specialist doctor called an anesthesiologist.

James Young Simpson tested chloroform on himself. It worked well!

CHLOROFORM

In 1847, Scottish doctor James Young Simpson pioneered the use of chloroform vapor to put people to sleep. He gave it to women in labor, to take away the pain of childbirth. One of the first people to use it was Queen Victoria. Chloroform was used until the early 1900s.

Using ether

Davy's assistant, Michael Faraday (1791–1867), discovered another gas, named ether, which had a stronger effect than laughing gas. In 1842 Crawford Long (1815–1878), a surgeon from Atlanta, Georgia, carried out a minor operation to remove cysts (lumps on the skin). His patient breathed ether to relieve pain. The Scottish surgeon Robert Liston (1794–1847) went further later that year. He gave a patient ether and cut off his leg in less than three minutes. The patient did not feel a thing!

Modern anesthetics

Ether is not used today. Modern "general anesthetics" render a patient unconscious so they cannot feel a thing until they wake up, while "local anesthetics" dull pain in just one area of the body.

Nursing

Nurses are important members of a modern medical team. They ensure the patient is getting better and is as comfortable as possible.

The founder of the nursing profession, Florence Nightingale, showed that good nursing helped people get better faster. In 1854, she led a team of 38 female nurses to care for soldiers wounded in the Crimean War (1853–1856; British, French and Turkish armies were fighting Russia.) Nightingale took over a

Florence Nightingale checked patients during the night. She became known as the "Lady with the Lamp."

FLORENCE NIGHTINGALE

Born into a rich English family in 1820, Florence Nightingale's mother did not want her to become a nurse. However, after her work in Turkey, Nightingale became a national hero. Nightingale died in 1910.

hospital in Istanbul, Turkey. Before her arrival most of the wounded died from diseases caught in the hospital. Nightingale ordered the hospital be cleaned, and her nurses made sure each patient was well looked after. The death rates dropped dramatically.

A women's profession

In 1860, Nightingale opened a training college for nurses in London, England. Nursing became one of the few professions open to women. In the United States at that time almost all nurses were men. That changed during the American Civil War (1861–1865). With many of the men fighting, women volunteered to be nurses in military hospitals. Dorothea Dix (1802–1887) was the chief nurse of the Union Army, organizing the care of thousands of wounded men on both sides.

> **FACTS**
> - Florence Nightingale was inspired to be a nurse after meeting Elizabeth Blackwell (1821–1910), the first woman doctor in the United States.
> - Before professional nurses, hospital patients were looked after by nuns or monks.

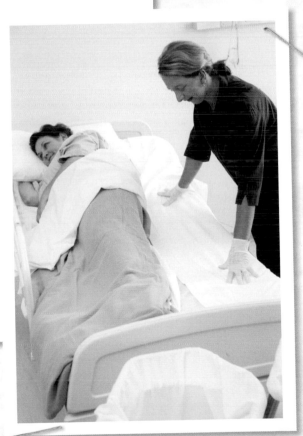

A nurse changes bed sheets while the patient is still in bed, so she stays comfortable even when too sick to get out of bed.

Germ Theory

In the 1860s, it was discovered that diseases and infections are caused by microorganisms, or germs. This idea is called the "germ theory."

Bacteria were first identified in 1676 and 200 years later, some were found to cause diseases.

Before the arrival of modern medicine, infectious diseases, such as cholera and bubonic plague (or Black Death), were a serious risk. Epidemics, or large outbreaks of disease, were common, especially in crowded cities. No one knew how the diseases spread. People thought they were carried by "bad air." By the 1850s it was becoming clear that many diseases were linked to hygiene, or cleanlinesss.

Louis Pasteur at work in his laboratory.

LOUIS PASTEUR

Born in France in 1822, Pasteur was a prolific researcher. As well as discovering germs, developing vaccines and food preservation, he found that light could be used to identify certain chemicals. Pasteur died in 1895.

External cause

In 1864, a French chemist called Louis Pasteur proved that food went bad because microscopic organisms were infecting it. He boiled up a broth, so that any bacteria or other "germs" in it were killed. The broth was placed in flasks. Some were sealed from the air; others were connected to the air via curved tubes or were simply left open. The sealed flasks did not spoil. The open flasks went bad first, while the curved necked flasks took a lot longer to go bad. Here was evidence that the cause of the decay came from germs carried in the air—it took longer for them to get in via the curved tubes.

Causing disease

Pasteur was also asked by the French silk industry to find out why their silkworms were dying of disease. He showed that the disease was caused by a protist (a tiny, single-celled organism). It could be eradicated by only letting healthy silkworms breed.

Pathogens

A German scientist Robert Koch (1843–1910) was an early expert on bacteria who showed that every disease is caused by a particular microorganism. He found a way of growing bacteria on a gel called agar that was made from seaweed. In 1876 he found that a rod-shaped bacterium causes anthrax (a disease of livestock and humans). He found the bacterium that causes tuberculosis (a lung disease) in 1882, and the bacterium that causes cholera (a digestive disease caught by drinking unclean water) in 1883. Organisms that cause disease were named pathogens.

IMPLICATIONS

Pasteur developed a process for keeping milk and other foods fresh without having to cook them. Known as pasteurization, it involves heating the food to a high temperature for a few seconds. That kills germs but does not alter the taste.

Milk stays fresh thanks to pasteurization but will go sour once germs are allowed into it.

Chilling food slows the growth of germs so the food will stay fresh for longer.

FACTS

- A refrigerator does not prevent all germs from growing. Food manufacturers add a date for when food becomes unsafe.
- Other pathogens include worms, fungus, viruses, and protists.

Anthrax and rabies

Pasteur made a vaccine for anthrax by heating the bacteria to create a non-deadly version. He tried the same with rabies, a disease of the nervous system. However, he could not grow the pathogen. We now understand that rabies is caused by a virus not a bacteria, and viruses do not behave in the same way.

Getting better

Germ theory led to improvements in public health. It showed that diseases could be prevented by proper sanitation and by keeping food fresh.

Washing hands is an easy way to prevent diseases from spreading.

19

Antiseptic

In the 1860s doctors began to use chemicals that could clean germs from wounds. These antiseptics saved many lives.

In the 19th century the importance of cleaning wounds was not understood. Small cuts could go septic (get infected with germs). To stop the infection the only thing to do was amputate (cut off) an arm or leg! Recently invented anesthetics helped make amputation easier, but patients often died of infections caused by the operation.

Joseph Lister wore neat and clean clothes to make sure he did not pass on germs to his patients.

JOSEPH LISTER

Lister was born in southern England in 1827. He chose carbolic acid as an antiseptic because it had been shown to kill pathogens in sewage. His first antiseptic operation was on a boy with a badly broken leg. Lister died in 1912.

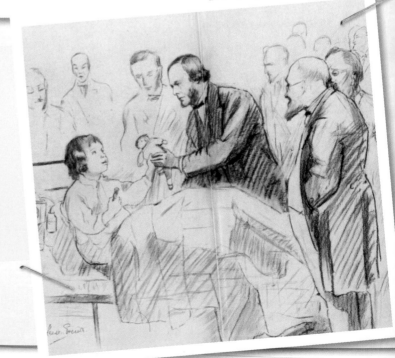

1865, Joseph Lister

20

Modern surgeons wash germs off their hands before operating and wear very clean clothes. Face masks stop doctors breathing germs on the patient.

Spraying acid

In 1865, Joseph Lister, an English surgeon, was the first doctor to use an antiseptic to make operations germ free. Lister washed wounds in carbolic acid during operations and wrapped them in tin foil to keep out germs. The acid burned the skin a little, so Lister switched to spraying a weaker acid onto a patient during operations. It prevented infections but made operating difficult.

Iodine is an effective antiseptic. It will kill any germs that get into a cut but does not damage the surrounding skin.

Aseptic conditions

Later surgeons preferred an aseptic approach. They operated in very clean rooms so no germs could reach the patient. This system is the one used today.

Talking Cures

In the 19th century, doctors assumed that mental illnesses were caused by problems with the brain. Sigmund Freud had other ideas.

Doctors who specialize in mental illnesses are known as psychiatrists. Early psychiatrists believed that all mental illness was caused by a physical problem with the brain. While some mental problems, such as dementia, where shown to be a physical problem, other illnesses had no obvious cause.

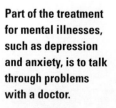

Part of the treatment for mental illnesses, such as depression and anxiety, is to talk through problems with a doctor.

Sigmund Freud believed that a person's mind was influenced by hidden, subconscious desires, and that mental illness was the result of a troubled subconscious.

In the mind

In 1885, a young Austrian psychiatrist called Sigmund Freud went to work in Paris under Jean-Martin Charcot (1825–1893). This Frenchman was a leading expert in the structure of the brain, and it was he who suggested to Freud that mental illness was a disturbance of the mind, not damage to the brain. (The mind is a person's thoughts and emotions, which are produced by the brain, but not necessarily controlled by it.)

Psychoanalysis

Freud began using psychoanalysis on patients. He believed that the mind was controlled by the subconscious—a collection of desires and urges that make a person behave in a certain way without really knowing why. Freud's treatment involved patients talking about their childhood, their dreams, and their anxieties, as a way of revealing problems hidden in their subconscious. In the same way, doctors treat mental illness today by talking about problems in the mind. It is also common for patients to be given drugs, and sometimes both treatments are used.

SIGMUND FREUD

Born in 1856 in what is now part of the Czech Republic, Sigmund Freud spent most of his life in Vienna, Austria. In 1938, Austria came under the control of Nazi Germany. Being Jewish, Freud was forced to flee to London, England, where he died the following year.

X-rays

In the 1890s an invisible form of radiation called X-rays was found that could take pictures of the inside of a living body.

Before X-ray scans allowed doctors to look inside a body without having to embark on risky surgery, the only way to figure out what was happening inside a patient was to check the outside of the body, take samples of blood and other things,

X-ray images show the hard objects, such as bones, that are under the skin.

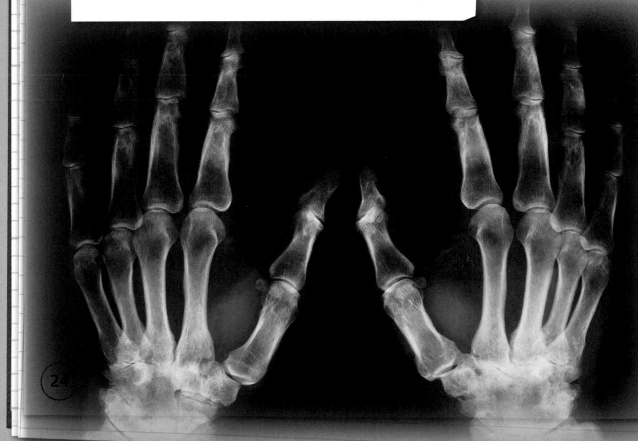

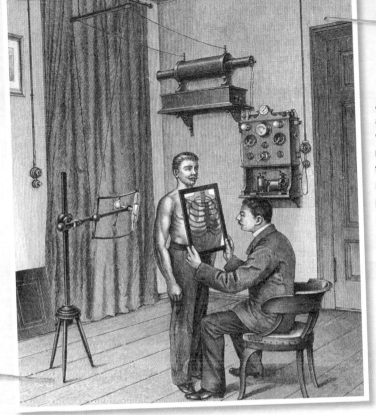

An X-ray scan is safe for a patient but healthcare workers who perform many tests must protect themselves from the rays—something that early practitioners did not know.

FACTS

- X-rays carry more energy than visible light so they can pass through more substances.
- A regular X-ray scan exposes you to less radiation than you receive while making a two-hour airplane flight.
- X-rays are used to check bones, teeth, and lungs.

or listen to the noises it made. In 1816, French physician René Laënnec (1781–1826) invented a listening tube, which amplified the body's sounds. This later evolved into the stethoscope, still used by doctors today. This helped doctors investigate the heart, lungs, and digestive system, but many more body parts did not make any sounds at all.

Chance discovery

In 1895 a German-born Dutch physicist named Wilhelm Röntgen discovered X-rays by chance. He was investigating the way electricity could make rays, and he discovered that photographic paper, which goes black when light shines on it, was affected in the same way by an invisible beam coming from his apparatus.

WILHELM RÖNTGEN

Born in 1845, Röntgen was a physicist working in Germany when he made his discovery of X-rays. In 1901 he was the first winner of the Nobel Prize for physics, set up that year to celebrate achievements in science. Röntgen died in 1923. In 2004 element 111 was named roentgenium in his honor.

Although he was a physicist, Röntgen is regarded as the founder of radiology, the science of medical scanning.

X-ray vision

Most amazingly of all, the rays—Röntgen called them X-rays because they were so mysterious—could pass through solid objects. When Röntgen directed a beam of X-rays through his wife's hand, he found it created a picture of the bones under her skin. The medical applications of these X-ray images was obvious straight away. In 1896, the first X-ray department was set up at a hospital in Glasgow, Scotland. In 1898 the British Army was using a mobile X-ray unit in Sudan to find bone fractures in injured soldiers before surgeons operated on them.

X-ray images

Soft substances, such as skin and muscles, do not block X-rays. The radiation just passes straight through and darkens the photo-sensitive plate behind. However, harder substances such as bone block the rays, so these objects cast a shadow on the plate, which reveal any problems with the bone, such as fractures.

Better view

In 1972 X-ray and computer technology were combined to give a better view. Computerized tomography (CT) scans combine hundreds of X-rays taken from different angles to build up a picture detailed enough to detect cancers and blood clots.

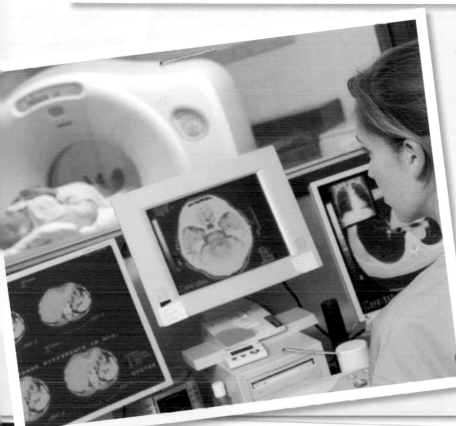

IMPLICATIONS

X-rays were the first medical scanner. Today's hospitals have a number of scanners for looking at different body parts. Scanners have made it possible to diagnose serious illnesses much more quickly.

A CT scanner images slices of the body, which can be combined to create a 3D view.

27

Painkillers

Today there are many medicines that can take away pain. In the 1890s, aspirin became the first mass-produced painkiller.

A simple pill can take away the pain of a headache. However, it won't cure whatever caused the pain.

Painkillers have been used since ancient times. One of the most powerful was opium, a form of heroin derived from poppy flowers. However, using such powerful painkillers was bad for the health. Other traditional painkillers also came from plants. For example, people chewed willow bark or drank tea made from meadowsweet leaves.

Chemical discoveries

In the 1820s it was found that a chemical in both willow and meadowsweet called salicylic acid could reduce pain and stop

FACTS

- Native Americans used slug slime to numb their mouths when they had a toothache.
- Aspirin is often used to reduce the risk of strokes.
- Aspirin has been found to cause a rare brain disease in children. People under 12 should not take aspirin.

swelling. In the 1850s people began to use it as a medicine. However, it gave patients a lot of stomach problems. In 1897, Felix Hoffman (1868–1946), a German chemist, found that a similar chemical—acetylsalicylic acid—worked just as well and did not hurt the stomach. In 1899 this drug was given the name aspirin.

Aspirin was the most popular painkiller until the 1980s, when people began to prefer acetaminophen.

Two types of painkiller

Aspirin is an anti-inflammatory drug. That means it acts at the site of the pain—a cut, for example—reducing the inflammation and weakening the pain response. Narcotics are more powerful painkillers that act on the brain, so the patient feels less pain all over the body. Narcotics, which include morphine, cause many side-effects and are used only in hospitals.

Willow bark is a natural source of a painkiller similar to aspirin.

Brain Waves

The nervous system sends electrical signals around the body. In 1924 a system was developed to monitor the brain's electrical activity.

Nerves carry messages around the body, connecting the senses to the brain, and the brain to the muscles. Messages are carried as a surge of electric charge— and a similar system is used to make muscles contract. As a result, body parts have a small electric field around them. In the early 20th century, doctors began to monitor these fields.

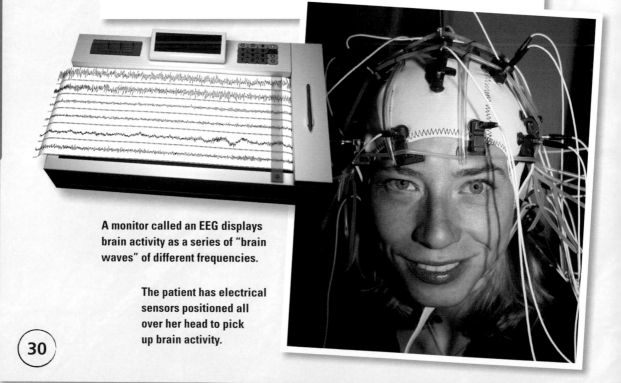

A monitor called an EEG displays brain activity as a series of "brain waves" of different frequencies.

The patient has electrical sensors positioned all over her head to pick up brain activity.

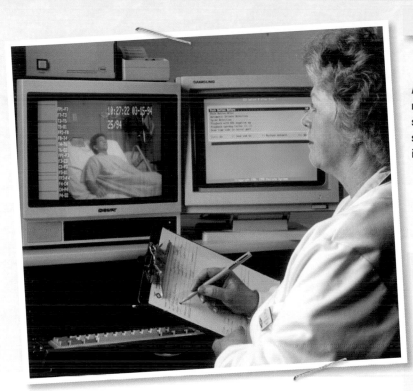

IMPLICATIONS

Electroencephalographs are useful for sleep research. For example, the changes in brain activity show how deeply a person is sleeping and when they are having a dream. This research has shown that we go through several 90-minute sleep cycles every night.

Electrical detectors

The first electrical monitor was the electrocardiograph (ECG). The ECG was invented by in 1903 by Dutch scientist Willem Einthoven (1860–1927). It records the electrical activity of the heart muscles. In 1924, German biologist Hans Berger (1873–1941) used a similar system for a electroencephalograph (EEG)—a brain monitor.

Brain activity

EEGs reveal a lot about a patient. Smooth, long electrical waves are called alpha waves. They show that a person is relaxed. Beta waves are more erratic and spiky. They are produced when a person is thinking hard. Long, slow delta waves show they are asleep. EEGs are used by doctors to diagnose epilepsy and other seizures. During these episodes, the brain activity shown on the EEG becomes jumbled.

Antibiotics

In the 1890s, the search began for a drug that kills germs attacking the body but doesn't harm the body itself. The answer was discovered by chance in 1928.

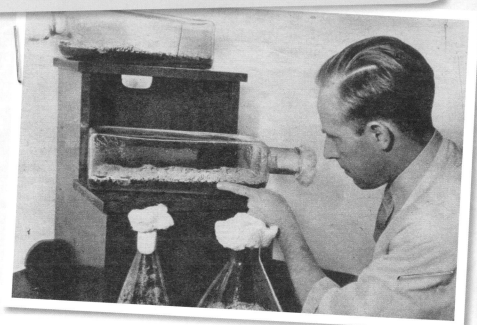

Alexander Fleming looks at mold growing in jars. This mold was the source of the first antibiotic, penicillin.

In the 1890s Paul Ehrlich (1854–1915), a German expert in bacteria, suggested that it might be possible to develop drugs that target germs invading the human body but leave body cells alone. His Japanese assistant Sahachiro Hata (1873–1938) tested over 600 chemicals before finding the one that could do the job. This substance was called Salvarsan, and in 1910 it was sold as the first antibacterial drug.

Penicillin tablets are made by extracting the antibiotic chemical from molds grown in factories.

Needing alternatives

However, Salvarsan treatment was very painful. For the drug to work properly, large amounts had to be injected. The search continued for a "magic bullet"—a simple treatment that only attacked germs. In 1928, a Scottish bacteriologist Sir Alexander Fleming (1881–1955) discovered that a fungus was able to kill bacteria, but he did not think it would be useful as a medicine. Instead a new set of antibacterial drugs began to be used.

Sulfa drugs

In 1932 the German Gerhard Domagk (1895–1964) discovered that a red dye called prontosil could also kill the bacteria that cause blood poisoning. In the late 1930s researchers developed a range of related drugs (called sulfonamides, or sulfa drugs) that were effective against bacterial diseases. Sulfa drugs became the main treatment for bacterial diseases until the late 1940s, when the first true antibiotic, penicillin, was introduced for public use.

Accidental discovery

Penicillin is a drug derived from the same fungus observed by Fleming. The fungus was a mold called *Penicillium notatum*, and Fleming had discovered its bacteria-killing effects by chance. He was growing infectious bacteria in his lab and left his sample while taking a summer-long vacation. After he returned he found mold growing on the samples. He noticed that was no bacteria growing in the area around the fungus.

IMPLICATIONS

Some of the first people to get penicillin were soldiers wounded in the last years of World War II (1939–1945). Without the antibiotic, many more soldiers would have died from infections.

Medics gave antibiotics to wounded soldiers being evacuated from the battlefield.

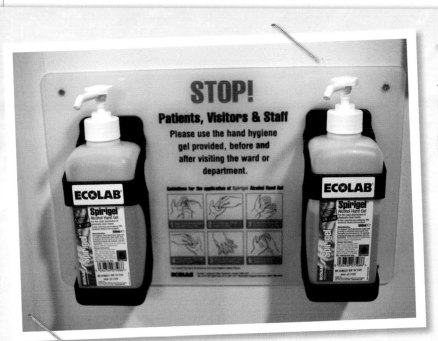

These hospital hand cleaners use a gel containing strong alcohol to kill germs.

SUPERBUGS

Some bacteria have become resistant to antibiotics and can cause dangerous infections. To prevent them spreading, everyone arriving at a hospital is expected to wash their hands.

Antibiotic

He reasoned that the fungus was releasing a chemical that stopped the bacteria from growing. He was right: the fungus produces a chemical—he named it penicillin for the fungus—that does not kill bacteria but stops them growing. (Other drugs, like sulfas, actively kill at least some of the germs.)

Purification

Fleming showed that penicillin could be used to treat infections but took the research no further. By 1944 Australian Howard Florey (1898–1968) and German Ernst Chain (1906–1979), working in the United States, had found a way of making pure penicillin. Today, penicillin is used to treat a wide range of infections, and many more antibiotics have been developed, mostly from different fungi.

Contraception

Methods for preventing pregnancy are known as contraception. In 1939, a way of producing a contraceptive pill was discovered.

Contraception has been practiced for centuries. Ancient Egyptians used pessaries (substances placed in the vagina) made of honey and crocodile dung. This concoction killed sperm entering the vagina, but was rather unpleasant.

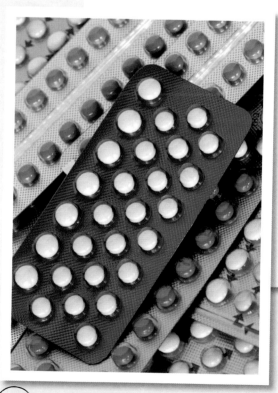

Forming a barrier

In the 1550s Italian Gabriello Fallopius (1523–1562) invented a cloth condom, which formed a barrier between partners and stopped sperm from getting to the uterus. (Modern rubber ones work far better.) The diaphragm, or cap, invented in the 1820s, does the same thing.

Most contraceptive pills are taken every day for three weeks, followed by a break for a week.

The contraceptive pill allows women to control how many children they have. Most American women have one or two kids.

Copying the body

Pregnant women produce the hormone progesterone. Its role is to stop the ovaries from releasing fresh eggs. The contraceptive pill contains a synthetic form of progesterone and stops non-pregnant women from ovulating (producing eggs) so they cannot become pregnant.

Artificial hormone

In 1939 American chemist Russell Marker (1902–1995) had found a way of making progesterone from a chemical in yams. Over the next 20 years this technology was used to create the first contraceptive pills. The pills used by women today work in the same way. Three quarters of American women take them at some point in their lives.

IMPLICATIONS

Unlike condoms, contraceptive pills provide no physical barrier between partners, and so do not protect against sexually transmitted diseases (STDs), such as HIV and syphilis. STDs have been becoming more common since the 1950s. Doctors advise people to use condoms to protect themselves from disease.

Condoms not only prevent pregnancy but also reduce the risks of spreading disease.

37

Ultrasound

In the 1950s a very safe way of looking inside the body was developed. Instead of radiation it used high-pitched sound.

1949, John Wild

X-ray scans are very safe, but there are some parts of the body that cannot be scanned in this way. Body parts where cells are dividing cannot be X-rayed. Any damage caused by the powerful rays would have a big impact as the cells continue to grow in number. Sex organs, the ovaries, and testes cannot be X-rayed for this reason, and neither can babies growing inside their mothers.

Using sound

Safer scans use ultrasound. Sounds are vibrations in the air, which our ears can detect. Ultrasound is the same kind of vibration, or wave, but it is so high-pitched that no animal can hear it. The sound

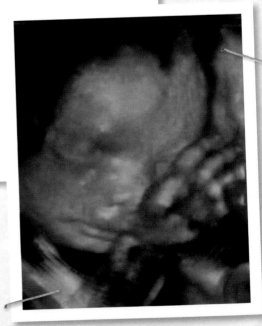

The latest ultrasound scans can show developing babies in three-dimensional images.

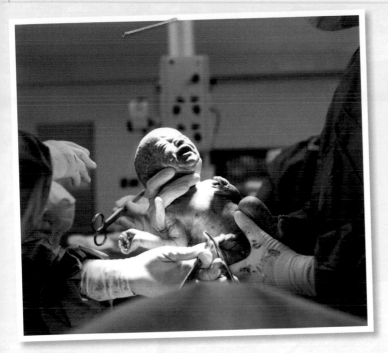

IMPLICATIONS

Babies are normally born head first. Coming out in other ways makes the birth more dangerous. Ultrasound scans alert doctors to these problems before labor starts. Often the safest option is a cesarian section, where a surgeon delivers the baby through a cut in the abdomen and uterus.

A baby being born by cesarian section. A third of all American babies are born this way.

waves are produced by a handheld speaker, or transducer, and the waves spread out through the skin, fat, and muscle of the body. They bounce off small objects, creating an echo, which is picked up by the transducer. A computer then uses the echoes to create an image. As well as being safe, ultrasound scans can detect soft objects, unlike X-rays.

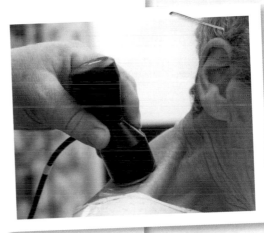

As well as scans, ultrasound is used to vibrate sore muscles, helping them relax.

Pioneering work

In 1949, the American doctor John Wild (1914–2009) used ultrasound to measure the thickness of an intestine. This was the first ultrasound scan. In the 1950s the first scans of babies on the uterus were made in Scotland. Today ultrasound is also used to soothe muscles and break up hard blockages inside the body.

Stem Cells

The human body grows from a single cell. Stem cell medicine is researching ways of using this growth system to repair damaged body parts.

1968, Robert Good

The body starts out as a single cell called a zygote. The zygote divides in two and carries on dividing into a ball of cells. As the cells divide they specialize to make up different parts of the body. This process is called differentiation. After a cell has differentiated, it can never change back. When it divides it will only produce more of the same type of cell.

A zygote, the first stem cell in a body, is formed when a sperm and egg cell merge together.

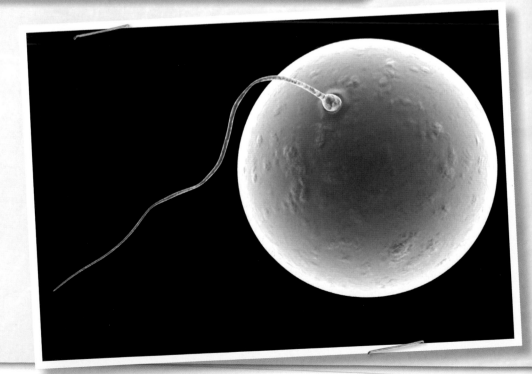

Rebuilding blocks

Undifferentiated cells are known as stem cells. As they divide, they can convert into any differentiated cell type. Doctors are searching for ways to use stem cells to rebuild damaged body parts. Stem cells are difficult to collect from a body, so research has focused on switching differentiated cells back into stem cells.

Bone marrow

The only widespread stem cell treatment currently performed is bone-marrow transplants. Stem cells from a donor are used to rebuild the blood supply of another person. The first bone-marrow transplant was carried out by American Robert Good (1922–2003) in 1968. New stem cell treatments are being tested and may become standard practice in the future.

FACTS

- Stem cell treatments might be used to correct genetic problems by introducing new genes to body parts.
- A zygote is totipotent—it can become any cell. Pluripotent stem cells are only able to convert into the cells needed to make one organ of body system.

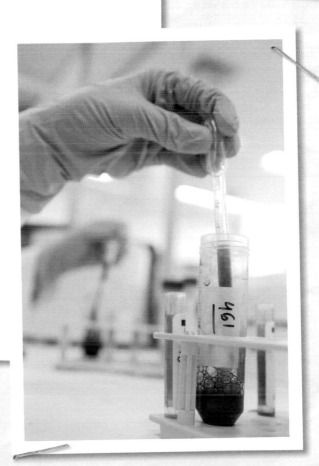

Stem cells in bone marrow produce red blood cells. During a transplant, they are injected into the bones of the patient.

MRI Scans

An entirely new medical imaging system was invented in 1977. MRIs gave the best view yet of the inside of a patient's body.

In 1977 the American physicist Raymond Damadian built the first MRI machine. It takes pictures using a technique called magnetic resonance imaging. MRI does not involve X rays or radioactive substances like earlier scanners, and it gives clear pictures of soft tissue. It can also be used to watch body parts in action, and produce live images of the brain. However, MRI machines are very expensive, so only large hospitals have them.

A functional MRI (fMRI) scan shows activity taking place in different parts of the brain

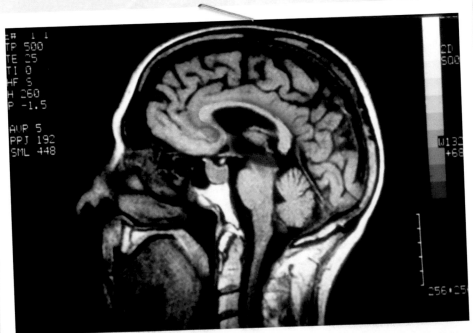

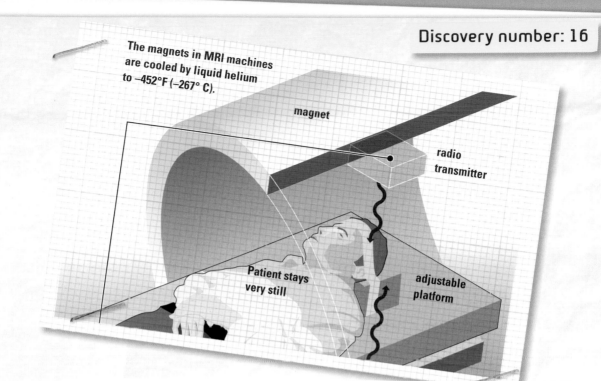

The magnets in MRI machines are cooled by liquid helium to −452°F (−267° C).

magnet

radio transmitter

Patient stays very still

adjustable platform

How it works

Magnetic resonance imaging makes use of the way hydrogen atoms resonate (vibrate) and give off radio waves when they are placed in a strong magnetic field. The patient lies on a platform inside what is basically a massive, hollow magnet. The magnet makes all the hydrogen atoms, which are in nearly every body chemical, line up to it—in the same way a compass lines up north to south. The scanner fires radio waves through the body. These make the atoms wobble and emit other radio waves. The scanner picks up the signals from the body, and uses them to create an image of the tissues.

IMPLICATIONS

Functional MRI (fMRI) scanners can track blood flow by picking up oxygen moving around the body. fMRIs are used to watch the brain in action. When a part of the brain is working, extra blood rushes into it—showing up on the scan. fMRIs are used to research consciousness—how the human mind thinks and feels emotions.

Test-tube Babies

Some couples cannot have children because of problems with the sexual organs. In 1979, a system for producing babies in a lab was perfected.

To make a baby, a sperm from the father needs to merge with an egg from the mother. This process, known as fertilization, happens naturally inside the mother a few hours after sexual intercourse. If fertilization cannot happen naturally, doctors can carry it out *in vitro*, which means "in glass." Sperm and eggs are mixed in a lab. The fertilized egg or embryo is then put back into the mother to grow as normal. Babies conceived this way are named "test-tube babies."

During IVF, sperm can be injected into an egg to produce fertilization.

1. Zygote divides in vitro

3. Fetus develops as normal

4. Baby born naturally

The first few days of the baby's development take place in vitro. It is then put into the uterus.

2. Embryo added to uterus

Infertility

There are many reasons why couples are infertile, or cannot have children naturally. The woman's fallopian tubes may be blocked, or sometimes mucus (thick, slimy fluid) in the cervix kills the man's sperm. Or, the man may produce relatively few sperm, or those that he does produce are defective in some way. In 1979, the IVF process was developed to help these couples become parents.

Louise Brown

IVF, which stands for "in-vitro fertilization," was pioneered by the British Patrick Steptoe (1913–1988) and Robert Edwards (1925–2013). The first test-tube baby—Louise Brown—was born in July 1978. Since then more than four million babies have been conceived by IVF.

IMPLICATIONS

During IVF, doctors often put more than one embryo into the mother. Often only one will survive, but occasionally all of them do well and are born together. Thanks to IVF, the number of twins or triplets has gone up in recent years.

Multiple births, such as these triplets, born through IVF are always non identical.

TIMELINE

600 BCE: Sushruta writes the first manual for surgeons.

1628 CE: William Harvey figures out how the heart pumps blood around the body.

1796: Edward Jenner makes a scientific test of a vaccine.

1799: Humphry Davy discovers the anesthetic effects of nitrous oxide gas.

1854: Florence Nightingale demonstrates the importance of good nursing.

1864: Louis Pasteur discovers that infections are caused by bacteria and other germs.

1865: Joseph Lister pioneers the use of antiseptics to prevent infections after surgery.

1885: Sigmund Freud begins his development of psychoanalysis.

1895: Wilhelm Röntgen discovers that X-rays can image internal body structures.

1897: Felix Hoffman develops the aspirin, an artificial form of a natural painkiller found in willow and other plants.

1924: Hans Berger invents the electroencephalograph, a device for measuring the electrical activity of the brain.

1928: Alexander Fleming discovers the germ-killing effects of a fungus. The chemical responsible is called penicillin, which becomes the first antibiotic.

1939: Russell Marker discovers a way of making artificial female hormones, which are used in contraceptive pills.

1949: John Wild invents ultrasound scans.

1968: Robert Good performs the first stem cell therapy with a bone-marrow transplant.

1977: Raymond Damadian invents the MRI machine for imaging soft tissues.

1979: Louise Brown, the first person conceived through IVF, is born in England.

GLOSSARY

Artery: A blood vessel that carries blood away from the heart.

Atom: A single unit of a substance.

Bacteria: A microscopic life form.

Cell: The smallest unit of a living body.

Dementia: A disease that damages the mind.

Epilepsy: A disease that causes the body to become uncontrollable.

Epidemic: A disease that affects a large number of people at once.

ER: A hospital Emergency Room.

Intestine: A section of the digestive system where nutrients and water are absorbed by the body.

Organism: Another word for a living thing.

Profession: A job that requires specialist training.

Protist: A microscopic lifeform.

Sanitation: A system for supplying clean water and taking away dirty water.

Subconscious: Part of the mind that is hidden.

Transplant: When a new body part is introduced by surgery.

Vapor: A gas.

Vein: A blood vessel that brings blood to the heart.

Unconscious: Being in a state of unawareness, similar to sleep.

Zygote: The first cell of a body.

FOR FURTHER READING

BOOKS

Allman, Toney. *Medieval Medicine and Disease.* San Diego, CA: ReferencePoint Press, Inc., 2015.

Davies, Gill. The Illustrated Timeline of Medicine. New York: Rosen Publishing, 2011.

Rogers, Kara (editor). Medicine and Healers Through History. Britannica Educational Publishing, 2011.

WEB SITES

Because of the changing nature of Internet links, Rosen Publishing has developed an online list of websites related to the subject of this book. This site is updated regularly. Please use this link to access this list:

http://www.rosenlinks.com/SCIB/Med

INDEX